KRAV MAGA

QuickStart Guide

The Simplified Beginner's Guide To Krav Maga

table of contents

BEFORE YOU START READING, DOWNLOAD YOUR FREE DIGITAL ASSETS!

Be sure to visit the URL below on your computer
or mobile device to access the free digital asset files
that are included with your purchase of this book.

These digital assets will compliment the material
in the book and are referenced throughout the text.

DOWNLOAD YOURS HERE:

www.clydebankmedia.com/kravmaga-assets

introduction

Krav Maga is an Israeli martial art born of necessity and brutal pragmatism. Its distinguishing characteristics include the continuous and synchronous combination of both offensive and defensive maneuvers, a no-holds-barred street fighting aesthetic, and a relatively easy learning curve that allows for quick and effective training. The system's fundamentals are extremely teachable, with new students learning highly effective techniques in a span of two to three lessons.

Some contend that the lack of ceremony found in Krav Maga warrants its reclassification from "martial art" to "military combat system." Unlike other martial arts, there is little emphasis on style, **Kata**, or spirituality. Instead, Krav Maga emphasizes the quick and efficient neutralization of enemy threats as well as effective techniques to deploy against armed assailants. To support the change further, the Israeli Defense Forces and other professional security and military organizations have used it to quickly prepare personnel for the possibility of hand-to-hand combat. Like martial arts, an emphasis on conflict avoidance does permeate the teachings of Krav Maga in civilian training environments, but this seems mainly to punctuate how brutal and extravagantly violent Krav Maga tactics can be, a force so deadly, it should only be used as a last resort.

Several organizations within Israel and elsewhere teach Krav Maga, both to military, security, and civilian forces, including Krav Maga Global (KMG), the International Krav Maga Federation (IKMF), and International Krav Maga (IKM). Certain Krav Maga organizations led by highly renowned instructors operate only in Israel. These organizations include IKMA (Israeli Krav Maga Association), KMF (Krav Maga Federation), and Bukan. For serious Krav Maga students, journeying to Israel to commence study or to perfect one's skills is viewed as a rite of passage.

Most Krav Maga organizations use a grading system based on three main categories, P, G, and E, which stand respectively for Practitioner, Graduate, and Expert. Each category is divided into 5 ranks. The five Practitioner levels account for the majority of

Krav Maga students worldwide. After mastering all of the essential techniques at the Practitioner level, students begin the five Graduate levels. A Graduate level ranking allows opens up the opportunity to become a Krav Maga instructor, though Graduates still need to pass a special instructor's course in order to do so. In many of the Israeli clubs, ranking is displayed using a standard colored belt ranking system based on Judo. Other organizations use patches to delineate one rank from another. Lines on the patch represent each rank within a category. For example, this patch *(figure 1)* signifies a fourth level ranking in the Practitioner category or "P4".

fig. 1 - P4 Patch

In order to qualify for Expert level ranking in Krav Maga, only those who prove themselves highly proficient in all Practitioner and Graduate level techniques and be outstanding overall fighters. Expert level Krav Maga instructors are most often chosen to teach military and security personnel. The highest ranking in Krav Maga is that of Master. Only a few people worldwide hold this title. A Master ranking essentially requires spending a lifetime developing expertise in Krav Maga and contributing significantly to the promotion and development of the Krav Maga fighting style.

As a disclaimer, it's important for the aspiring Krav Maga fighter to understand what this book *can* and *cannot* provide. This book *can* provide sound insight into the fundamental principles and philosophy of Krav Maga. It can serve as a primer for training and give a significant advantage over individuals with no knowledge whatsoever about the Krav Maga fighting style. *The book cannot train the fighter – only a certified trainer can.* None of the techniques illustrated and described in the book should be relied upon in a combat situation unless the situation is supervised and instructed by a graduate level Krav Maga fighter.

chapter one
HISTORY

The story of Krav Maga begins with the story of one man. Imi Lichtenfeld was a gifted Jewish athlete who grew up in a difficult part of the world during a difficult time. Born in 1910, Imi's childhood home was pre-World War II Czechoslovakia, or present day Slovakia. He was an accomplished wrestler, gymnast, and boxer, winning several national and international awards and competitions.

By the mid-1930s, violent anti-Semitism plagued Czechoslovakia. Jewish communities were in peril, regularly harassed and assaulted. Lichtenfeld sought refuge in the expansive study of martial arts, namely Judo and Jujutso. It soon became apparent to Imi that the point scoring systems of traditional martial arts competitions just didn't correlate well, physically or mentally, with the reality of street violence. This realization led Lichtenfeld to organize a group of boxers and wrestlers together to develop a real-world, practical fighting technique that emphasized a no-holds-barred, survivalist method to neutralize *attackers*, armed or unarmed.

By 1940, as Nazi power continued to expand in Czechoslovakia and globally, Lichtenfeld decided to relocate to Palestine to join the Zionist movement. In 1942 he joined the Haganah, a pre-Israel security force charged with protecting settlers who were relocating to the region. Lichtenfeld's penchant for and knowledge of hand-to-hand combat quickly caught the attention of his superiors, and he was soon placed in charge of the military's elite fighting forces, including the elite strike force, Palmach, and the Palyam, which were similar to marine commandos.

Israel gained statehood in 1948, and the Haganah, Palmach, and Palyam were combined into one defensive body known as the Israeli Defense Forces. Lichtenfeld was named Chief Instructor of Physical Fitness and assigned to conduct his operations at the IDF School of Combat Fitness. After over a decade of chaos and violence, Lichtenfeld finally had a relatively secure setting in which to institutionalize and refine the combat system that had been born out of necessity. Keeping the ruthless, ascetic qualities of the system intact, Lichtenfeld named his system "Krav Maga," or "Contact Combat" in Hebrew. He was determined not to mellow out his system in the wake of peace time but to retain the spirit of struggle and visceral desperation born of a people fighting back against the threat of extinction. In the years to come, Lichtenfeld would spawn a lineage of Krav Maga fighters and instructors, and the fighting system would be enshrined as one of the world's deadliest and most efficient martial arts.

chapter two
PRINCIPLES

In 1935, long before he joined the Haganah, Imi Lichtenfeld visited Paletine to compete in the Maccabi games as a wrestler. Unfortunately, an injury he sustained while training resulted in a broken rib and prohibited Imi from competing in the games. Imi's frustration led to one of the basic principles of Krav Maga, "do not get hurt" while training.

Philosophically, Krav Maga is less limited than other martial arts. The overarching goal for Krav Maga students is to cultivate a mentality of awareness and street smarts that can be relied upon in the heat of a real life-threatening situation. Consider Jiu Jitsu, also known for its emphasis on reality-based, practical self-defense. Jiu Jitsu emphasizes the principle that technique and skill can allow a smaller fighter to physically control and dismantle the offense of a larger or stronger *opponent*. The Jiu Jitsu fighter is trained to take her opponent to the ground where techniques can be employed to gain leverage and apply lethal submission holds. Krav Maga also trains the fighter to stay on her feet if there's a chance that the opponent has an accomplice who can simply stomp on the fighter's head during a ground scuffle. Rather than indulge in protracted *grappling*, wrestling, and scrambling for leverage, Krav Maga trains fighters to *neutralize threats as fast as possible*.

Rapid neutralization of threats is the most fundamental principle of Krav Maga. The ethos of efficiency trumps all others. The Krav Maga fighting environment assumes that every threat will ultimately kill you if given the chance, therefore you must thoroughly and unequivocally neutralize said threats by any means necessary, and you must proceed as quickly as possible to maximize your chances for survival in the face of multiple threats. There is no such thing as fighting etiquette in this system. For the sake of neutralization with maximum rapidity, fighters are trained to target the most vulnerable areas of the body such as the eyes, face, neck, throat, groin, solar plexus, ribs, knees, fingers, and feet. Other Krav Maga principles include:

SIMULTANEOUS OFFENSE & DEFENSE

In this martial art, there is no acceptable defense that doesn't include offense. Stemming from the ethos of neutralizing threats with maximum efficiency, Krav Maga has little tolerance for two-handed blocks or any other wholly defensive moves that occupy whole beats of the combat rhythm. Krav Maga fighters are taught to almost always block with one hand while attacking with the other.

SIMPLICITY

Part of Krav Maga's practicality is its quick learning curve. Krav Maga is composed of strikes, holds, and blocks, which can be taught very quickly. This doesn't mean that anyone can become a lethal fighting machine overnight, but a couple days of Krav Maga training can bestow life-saving fundamental self-defense skills.

CONTINUOUS MOTION

The concept of "retzev," Hebrew for continuous motion, also stems from the principle of fast neutralization. Training Krav Maga drills in efficient techniques for almost any close combat situation. The Krav Maga fighter should be able to execute techniques of maximum efficacy in a steady fluid sequence with no hesitation or second-guessing. You'll notice when watching Krav Maga in action that every attack from an adversary is met by a flurry of counterattacks, carefully placed to exploit the opponent's most vulnerable areas.

NOTE

Because Krav Maga techniques can be taught quickly, many military organizations around the world continue to incorporate it into their training systems.
E.g. Belgian Army, Polish Navy, Swedish Military, and the US Air Force Office of Special Investigations.

THE USE OF WEAPONS & ARMED OPPONENTS

Whether it's an AK-47 or a stick on the ground, the Krav Maga philosophy is: "If you've got 'em, use 'em." Much of Krav Maga training is devoted to the use of ***weapons*** in combat. Usually the training focuses on firearms, knives, bats and other blunt objects. Krav Maga also trains fighters to neutralize threats posed by armed opponents.

FOCUS ON THE BODY'S MOST VULNERABLE AREAS

Though some criticize Krav Maga for its encouragement of eye gouging, groin punching, and other not-so-gentlemanly (or lady-like) tactics, it's important to remember the fundamental Krav Maga ethos of neutralizing dangerous threats as quickly as possible. This is why many of Krav Maga's fighting tactics can result in permanent debilitating injury or even death to would-be assailants. There is no room for etiquette when a person's life hangs in the balance.

SUBDUING HOLDS

In addition to strikes, Krav Maga emphasizes several holds designed to subdue an opponent. Whether you're breaking bones or putting someone to sleep with a chokehold, as long as you fully neutralize the opponent quickly, then you're in line with the teachings of Krav Maga.

AVOIDING CONFLICT

Although Krav Maga is all about pragmatism and survival, there is an emphasis placed on avoiding conflict whenever it is possible to do so safely. This isn't Krav Maga's attempt at advancing an ethic of altruism and good will towards men, but a call for cool-headedness and sober decision-making in the face of a life-threatening circumstance. Krav Maga is about fighting for survival, not pride.

chapter three
WARM UP & BASICS

All warm up, stretching, and training for Krav Maga should be attempted under the supervision of an authorized instructor. The following descriptions will provide a technical outline of the skills you'll be learning but cannot account for the physiological and psychological nuances and varying degrees of physical fitness and skill level of the trainee.

The purpose of cardiovascular warm ups and stretching is to prepare your body for aerobic exercise and to minimize the risk of damage to your muscles. To prepare your body to train, start with two minutes of jumping jacks. Alternate throughout the two-minute period between jumping fast and jumping slowly. Follow the jumping jacks by running in place for a minute or so, just enough to get your body warmed up. Do some simple stretches of the arms, legs, and back.

When forming your fighting stance, it's important to position yourself in a way that assures maximum readiness for any attack, and though there's a limitless variety of situations you may encounter, a good basic fighting stance generally has a few constant features. Unlike other martial arts, which contain veritable catalogs of difference stances, Krav Maga keeps it simple with two stances: *neutral stance* and *fighting stance*. Keep your weight on the balls of your feet with your non-dominant foot leading your dominant foot. This

NOTE

Warm ups vary greatly depending on the participant's preexisting level of fitness. Work with your trainer to find a warm up routine that's appropriate for your level of fitness.

fig. 2 - Fighting Stance

NOTE

The front hand is used when striking with a jab.

way, you'll be able to deliver your strongest kick without having to reposition your feet. Keep your elbows down and bent so that your arms shelter your ribcage, and keep your chin tucked in so that if you do take impact on your head, it will be on your forehead. Bring your hands up to guard your face, making sure that your arms continue to shield your ribcage. This baseline stance, pictured below in *figure 2*, optimally prepares you to block, strike, or move away. Different environments call for different variations to your stance. Krav Maga is meant to help you respond to threats at any time and in any place. This includes confined spaces, stairways, inside cars, in an alley, or even in water. Different Krav Maga techniques are available for most any starting position—sitting down or lying down on your back, on your belly, or on your side.

THE CROSS BODY PUNCH

In Krav Maga, the contact point for a punch is either the top of the fist or the heel of the hand. Regardless of the weapon, the mechanics are the same. The weapon always leads the motion, followed by the body. For the cross body punch, pictured on the next page in *figure 3*, the weapon is the dominant hand, which is the rear hand in a standard fighting stance. During the cross body punch, a transfer of weight across the body lends force to the punch. To throw the cross body punch, make sure your chin is down, your shoulders are forward, and you're in a relaxed position. Keep your arm loose and relaxed as you throw the punch, and don't tighten your fist until just before the moment of contact. Contact should be made with the top two knuckles if you are using the top of your fist as your weapon. If your weapon is the heel of your hand, then adhere to the exact same mechanics while throwing the punch, and don't stiffen your arm and hand until just before impact. The palm heel strike actually allows for more power behind the punch and removes the strain to the wrist. The palm heel strike is the best choice to minimize risk of injury and is also the best choice for women with longer nails who have a harder time making a fist. While practicing the cross body punch, target different areas of your opponent of practice dummy's body. Rotate between striking the chest, the throat, and just above the mouth. Be sure to use quick and controlled weight transfers through your legs and hips to generate power for your punches. One way to practice this is to pivot the foot during the punch as if you were putting out a cigarette or stepping on a bug. Pivoting while you practice will force you into the habit of using your hip.

ELBOW STRIKES

fig. 3 – Cross Body Punch

Krav Maga gives much focus to close quarter combat situations. Being able to strike quickly and effectively with the elbow is of vital importance. There are seven different types of elbow strikes, known as elbows 1 through 7. Practicing the 7 elbow strikes is usually done in the neutral stance rather than the fighting stance. The neutral stance is used simulate and prepare responses for unexpected attacks, and seeing as effective elbow strikes can be executed without dramatic transfers of weight, they often provide your first line of defense when attacked by surprise.

THE SEVEN ELBOW STRIKES

1} HORIZONTAL ELBOW STRIKE

Cock the elbow back and swing forward to make contact with the opponent's head or chest. Use your body, mainly your hips, to power this movement, not just the arm.

2} HORIZONTAL BACKWARD ELBOW STRIKE

Using another quick stabbing motion, just your elbow back behind you, and attempt to make contact with your opponent's chest or head. Try to take a quick look before striking to avoid landing the strike with poor placement.

3} SIDEWAYS ELBOW STRIKE

Use this elbow strike to fend off opponents on your flank. With a stabbing motion, hut the elbow over the chest and strike out towards the outside flank. Be sure to keep the elbow parallel to your shoulders throughout the movement.

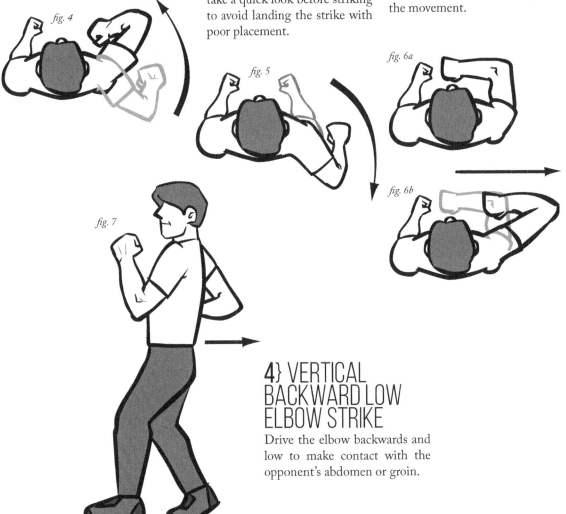

fig. 4

fig. 5

fig. 6a

fig. 6b

fig. 7

4} VERTICAL BACKWARD LOW ELBOW STRIKE

Drive the elbow backwards and low to make contact with the opponent's abdomen or groin.

5} VERTICAL BACKWARD HIGH ELBOW STRIKE

This is like a backwards uppercut using your elbow. Drive the elbow backwards from low to high and try to catch your opponent under his chin. This move will clear space for your next attack.

fig. 8

6} VERTICAL FORWARD & UPWARD ELBOW STRIKE

This strike is the opposite of #5. Again your goal is make contact underneath your opponent's chin and clear some room, but you're striking forward this time.

fig. 10

fig. 9

7} VERTICAL FORWARD & DOWN ELBOW STRIKE

This strike is punctuated by the full force of your body weight. Drive your elbow quickly up then back down like a hammer, making contact with the back of your opponent's head or back.

As you practice your elbow strikes, use the rotation of your torso and hips to generate power. Don't rely only on the swing of your arms. The ideal point of contact for an elbow strike is just below the tip of the elbow, on the outer reaches of the forearm. With the proper rotation of the body to provide power, well-placed elbow strikes can be huge equalizers when the opponent has a size or strength advantage. Elbow strikes can crush bone, cut skin, dislodge teeth and provide your opponent with any other odd form of violent debilitation. Practice your seven elbow strikes until you know which one to apply in any given situation without having to think about it.

UPPERCUT PUNCH

This attack is extremely useful when attempting to compromise an opponent's blocking. Usually targeting the chin or body, this punch is most effective at close range. As with most any other strike or kick in Krav Maga, full body movement is integral to a powerful offense. Since the movement of the uppercut is from low to high, you must use your legs properly to power this punch. For a right uppercut, the right leg should lift the body, slightly transferring the body weight through the punch and into the opponent. For an uppercut with the left hand, then the weight transfer will occur on the opposite leg but remain timed to coincide with the delivery of the punch. Like the cross body punch, the uppercut makes contact using the knuckles of the forefinger and the middle finger. Keep the hand that is not throwing the punch up near your face in a half-guard to protect against other attacks.

EYE STRIKES

Though strikes to the eye and groin are illegal in tournaments and discouraged in sport-based martial arts, they are integral to Krav Maga and can be extremely useful and even lifesaving in real self-defense situations such as attempted rape. Given that these techniques can permanently debilitate your opponent, they should only be used in a dire, life-threatening situation.

To perform an eye strike, attack at a slightly upward angle. If you try to come in at a straight angle or from the top down, you're more likely to make contact with the forehead in what will prove a useless attack. Coming up from below gives you a higher margin of error if your aim is a little off or if your opponent moves his head.

An eye strike is extremely useful if you're dealing with a bigger, more powerful opponent. If he is moving his arm towards you to strike or grab, counter with the eye strike, striking inside of his arm. This way you're thwarting his attack while executing your own. Stiffen your fingers right before the point of impact, making them as straight and as hard as possible.

JABS AND STRAIGHT PUNCHES

In a style like Krav Maga, with its emphasis on constant offense, your jab is a critical tool. Though a jab won't usually end a fight, it will put your opponents on defense and help you achieve the positioning necessary to deliver that world-shattering knockout blow.

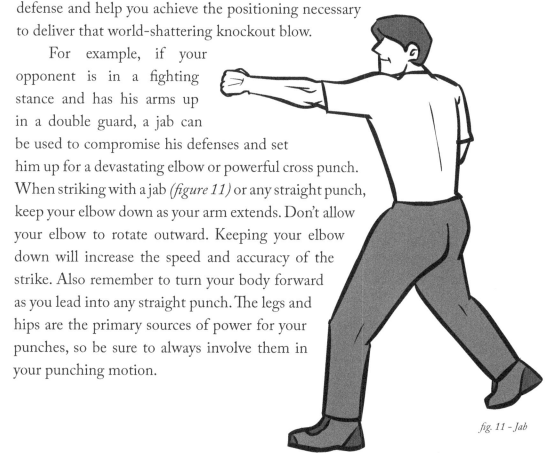

For example, if your opponent is in a fighting stance and has his arms up in a double guard, a jab can be used to compromise his defenses and set him up for a devastating elbow or powerful cross punch. When striking with a jab *(figure 11)* or any straight punch, keep your elbow down as your arm extends. Don't allow your elbow to rotate outward. Keeping your elbow down will increase the speed and accuracy of the strike. Also remember to turn your body forward as you lead into any straight punch. The legs and hips are the primary sources of power for your punches, so be sure to always involve them in your punching motion.

fig. 11 - Jab

THE HAMMER FIST

As its name implies, the hammer fist technique involves holding your fist vertically aligned with the ground as if you were clenching a hammer and striking with the outer heel pad, below the pinky. This technique can be used strategically to protect the fist or to strike more effectively within a close contact situation such as a grapple.

When throwing a hammer fist punch, the basic mechanics are the same as a straight punch. You want your shoulders relaxed and your non-punching hand close to your head in a half-guard. The movement of the hammer fist punch is forward and downward, either to strike at an enemy's chest area or to strike an enemy down further after he's been doubled over or otherwise vertically compromised. Just like with your straight punches, you should be rotating your hip as you throw the punch to generate maximum force.

When you practice the hammer fist punch on a pad or a practice dummy, strive to make contact with the exact same area of the target with both your left-handed and right-handed strikes. Doing so will help you train your hips to rotate and will help you control the aim and trajectory of your punches, which will be critical when you need to target the soft points on an opponent's body. For example, the hammer fist, if executed with enough strength and precision, can break an opponent's clavicle and leave him without the use of one arm. The hammer fist is also a great way to quickly split the *full guard* of an opponent who is in a fighting stance.

A common variation on the hammer fist is the "mouth of hand" strike, which is another close quarter offense. The mouth of hand attack uses the same fist and form as the hammer fist, but instead of striking downward you strike upward with the "mouth" of the hand—where the thumb wraps around the forefinger—usually in an effort to compromise the guard of an opponent and make contact with his chin. This technique is generally not as effective as the basic Krav Maga uppercut, which accomplishes the same end.

PALM HEEL STRIKES

Palm heel strikes use the meaty, bottom of the inner palm to make contact instead of the fist. The body mechanics involved in throwing the punch are the same as those involved in throwing straight punches. The actual power generated by a properly executed palm heel strike can be superior to that of a straight punch, because less force is wasted in the wrist when throwing a palm heel strike. Women in particular may not have the same amount of strength or stability in their wrists as do men, so palm heel strikes are often the ideal weapon for female fighters. Men who are just beginning to train in Krav Maga may find palm heel strikes easier to throw than straight punches due to the lessened impact on the wrists.

When using the palm heel strike, *(figure 12)* there should be a slight inward rotation of the wrist as the heel prepares for impact. Don't simply push your palm heel into the target, but place it strategically with a huge amount of force. As with straight or hammer fist punches, shoulders should be kept up with at least one arm forming a half-guard to protect the head. The chin should be tucked down, as always.

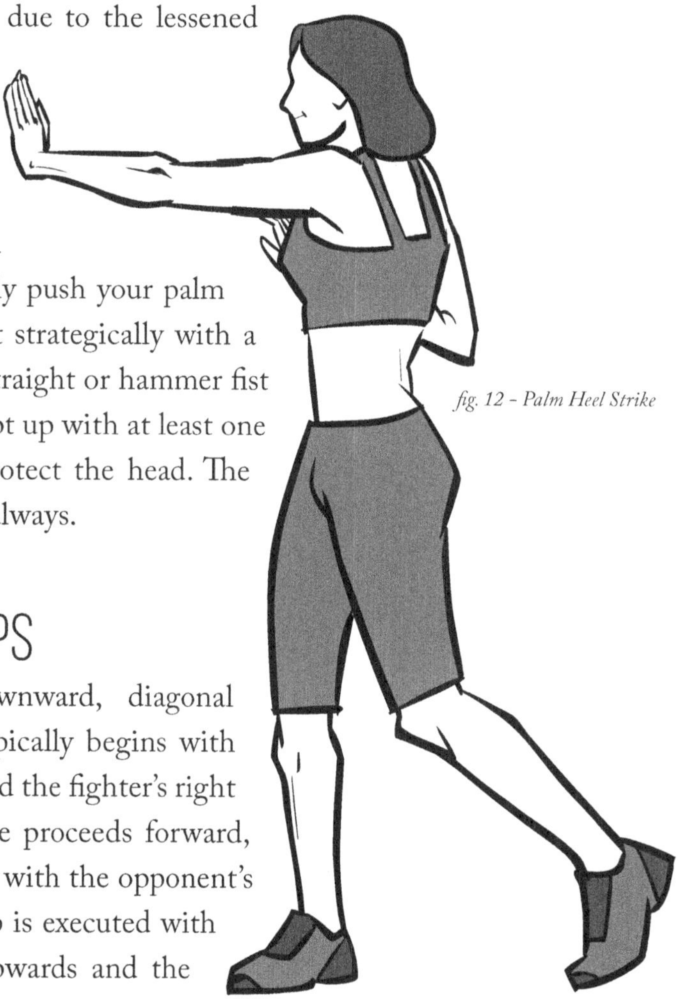

fig. 12 - Palm Heel Strike

OUTSIDE & INSIDE CHOPS

Outside chops have downward, diagonal trajectories. An ***outside*** chop typically begins with the arm raised across the body and the fighter's right hand near his left ear. The strike proceeds forward, down and across making contact with the opponent's neck or clavicle. An ***Inside*** Chop is executed with the palm of the hand facing upwards and the fighter swinging inwards toward the opponent's centerline, making contact with the neck or just above the mouth.

The best way to deliver a powerful chop is with "the knife hand." The knife hand is used in karate to form the famous "karate chop," and is in fact an extremely dangerous weapon. To form a lethal knife hand, start by opening your hand and raising the middle knuckles in all four of your fingers upward to create tension in the hand. Bend the thumb slightly and align it with the forefinger. Now you're ready to chop. Breath out as you strike downward or inward with the same hip and leg rotation you used for straight punches, hammer punches and palm heel strikes. As you close in on the target, tighten the wrist and pop the knife edge of the hand into direct contact with the target.

HEAD-BUTTS

A head-butt is another brutal weapon that can be used in close quarter combat or when your arms have been restrained.

To execute a head-butt, bring the crown of your head into contact with the opponent's face below the eye line. You can head-butt your opponent when standing face to face, from the side, or from the back. If executing a front head-butt, use the power in your legs rather than just whipping your neck forward. If your arms are free, then you can grab the opponent's shoulders and pull yourself forward into impact. Though they can be devastating, head-butts are often used simply to break a hold or to put some space between you and your opponent as you prepare for the next strike.

HOOK PUNCH

A well-placed hook punch is one of the best routes through an opponent's single or double guard. The hook punch also adheres nicely to the Krav Maga principle of simultaneous defense and offense, as the wide berth of the arm makes countering a hook difficult.

When executing a hook punch, there are two options for the angle of the fist: European or American style. The European technique holds the fist with the palm parallel to the ground at the end of the motion, so that if the thumb were to be extended, it would point towards the person throwing the punch. The American version of the hook ends with the palm perpendicular to the ground, so that the extended thumb would point upwards. For both styles it's important to swing the hip to generate power. You may either keep the foot planted or pivot it some—as if you were squashing a bug—to generate extra power.

The hook punch is executed with the leading hand and can be very dangerous, especially when the jab is used to position the opponent or compromise his guard.

chapter four
KICKS & KNEE ATTACKS

Many Krav Maga offensive techniques use the feet, legs and lower body. Kicks and knee attacks can be devastating offensively, but to execute they usually require more time and mental commitment than do punches. In this chapter we'll review some common kicks and knee attacks and discuss ways they can be applied in a combat situation.

BACK KICK

The back kick in Krav Maga is a basic and powerful weapon that can be used both defensively and offensively. It's a relatively quick attack to generate, pushing off your front-most foot, lifting your knee and thrusting straight backward with your striking foot, as if you were stomping horizontally through your opponent.

Be sure to aim your kick by looking laterally around your arm and not over your shoulder. If you aim by looking over your shoulder, then your body won't be crouched low enough to deliver the kick with maximum force.

The back kick is often the optimal defense to an *assailant* coming at you from behind. If this is your primary assailant, then you must rotate your body after delivering your kick to face your opponent in your fighting stance. With practice you can execute this kick and pivot quickly and fluidly.

If you want to use a back kick on an opponent in front of you, integrating it into a flurry of offense, then you can use your jab to buy yourself the time you need for a quick 180-degree pivot and kick. You don't even need to worry about turning your head if you're able to execute the sequence in less than a second. The best way to do this is to use a second jab or strike to accompany your spin. You don't even need to make contact with this strike, but force your opponent into a reaction that leads him to raise his guard higher, focusing on your hands, while exposing his midsection to your kick.

FRONT KICK

This kick, shown below in *figure 13*, is very simple and can traumatize your opponent since its primary target is the groin. This kick is a long-range weapon. You will need some space for your leg to swing. Your contact point will be the top of your shoelaces or the bottom of your shin. Start by getting into a fighting stance with your legs slightly bent, your back heel off the ground, and your chin tucked down. When you swing forward with your leg, generate the kick's power by swinging forward and away *and* by snapping your lower leg up and into the target. Breathe out as you kick.

If you are kicking to the groin, which is acceptable and even encouraged in Krav Maga, then you should not be looking toward that area. Your eyes can telegraph your intentions to your opponents. Looking down also compromises the power of your execution by leading you to prepare for impact and slowing down the end of your kick, as opposed to "kicking through" the target, assuring maximum velocity at the point of impact. Pretend you are trying to kick your opponent's head. Keep your eyes focused on the center of your opponent, where you can see both his arms and his legs. Be sure to lean into your kick with your hips. You should have your non-kicking foot raised slightly off its heel at the apex of your kicking motion. After completing your kick, pull your foot back and reconfigure your fighting stance as quickly as possible.

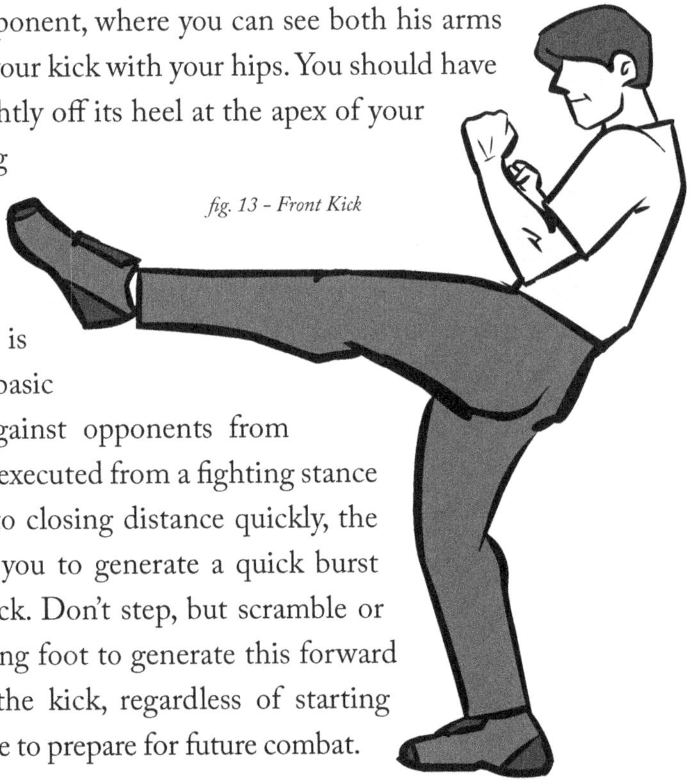

fig. 13 - Front Kick

The "advancing front kick" is an aggressive variation on the basic front kick that can be used against opponents from longer distances. this kick can be executed from a fighting stance *or* a neutral stance. In addition to closing distance quickly, the advancing front kick will allow you to generate a quick burst of momentum to power your kick. Don't step, but scramble or burst forward on your non-kicking foot to generate this forward momentum. After completing the kick, regardless of starting stance, go into your fighting stance to prepare for future combat.

SIDE KICK

The side kick usually targets a lower area like the knee and is harder for an opponent to catch than higher kicks, which target the ribs, chest, or face. The impact point is going to be the outer side of your heel, also known as the "blade" of your foot.

The mechanics of the side kick are very simple. Lift your kicking leg until your thigh is just higher than your waist, turn your kicking leg slightly forward as you thrust out. During your kicking motion, your ***base foot*** should pivot with the base foot's heel pointing towards the target at the end of the kicking motion. The side kick will improve with your training. Through routine and repetition you will master the transfer of weight and force through your body to execute a hard and well-controlled kick. You can practice your side kick using a four-step motion. The first step is lifting your leg, the second is thrusting forward, the third is returning your leg to your body, and the fourth is bringing your kicking foot back to the floor.

Keep an eye on your base foot when practicing the side kick, and make sure that you're turning it all the way. A lot of beginning Krav Maga students have a tendency to turn the base foot only 90 degrees rather than 180 degrees and end up struggling with their balance during the kick. A good way to begin practicing the side kick is by "pre-turning" your foot to the proper angle with the heel of your foot pointing towards the target. When you drill from this position, you can give full focus to the kicking motion. When you're comfortable with the kicking motion, you can integrate the pivot with the base foot.

ROUND KICK

The mechanics of the round (or roundhouse) kick in Krav Maga are similar to those of the front kick, at least in the beginning. Like other kicks, the ideal target for a round kick is the opponent's knee. If an opponent is able to grab your leg during a kick, he may be able to force you to the ground where you'll sacrifice much of your offensive ability. Also, the knee takes relatively few pounds of pressure to break, and once you do, the pain and mobility impairment will surely neutralize any threat your opponent poses.

The roundhouse kick begins the same way as the front kick, but instead of extending the leg straight and forward, you're going to create an angle that allows your leg to come in from the side. Raise your knee at the beginning of the motion, then pivot with your base foot and rotate your leg around to make contact with your opponent's knee.

VERTICAL FRONT KICK

The vertical front kick *(figure 14)* is different from the standard front kick in that the ball of the foot (just under the toes) is used as the impact point. Also, rather than the groin, the target of the vertical front kick is the belt buckle or belly. The objective of the vertical front kick is to push your opponent back. Consider a multi-attacker scenario. A nicely-placed vertical front kick to an assailant could be used to buy yourself some time to deal with other assailants in the party, or it could be used to push an assailant over a ledge or into an object or another opponent. Not to mention, it hurts.

To execute the vertical front kick, you'll need to follow the same

fig. 14 - Vertical Front Kick

body mechanics when executing the front kick, but lift your foot a little higher and strike with the ball of your foot. A lot of beginners struggle with this impact point. It can be difficult to get your toes back far enough to avoid making impact with them. You can train yourself to avoid this mistake in your spare moments using a wall to stretch your toes. Place your feet up against a wall and simply pull your toes up and away from the surface while pushing in with the heel of your foot. This may be a little difficult to do if you have really hard shoes, so do this exercise either barefoot or with soft shoes (like wrestling shoes). You can also generate good muscle memory by making a habit of tapping your toes on the ground. Finally, you can drill using a suspended heavy bag, extending your leg, bending your toes back and repetitively striking forward with the ball of your foot, just to get used to the awkward way of making impact.

LEG SWEEP

The leg sweep can be used to quickly bring an opponent to the ground. To perform an efficient leg sweep, the first thing you want to do is distract your opponent so you can properly position yourself to execute the sweep. You can distract your opponent with a jab, or by grabbing them by the neck or face, anything that will take his focus away from your legs.

Position your body within a foot of your opponent with both legs squared vertically with your shoulders. If your opponent's left leg is more vulnerable, then use your left leg to cross through and behind your opponent's leg, hook it, and pull outwards with your leg to force your opponent off balance and onto the ground.

UPPERCUT BACK KICK

Another close quarter tactic is the uppercut back kick, which can be used to attack an assailant who is at your rear. The move works best when you can generate a little bit of momentum going upwards into the kick. If you can bend your knees a little and spring upwards while you launch your kick, then do so. The target for the uppercut back kick is usually the groin. This is not a very powerful kick and usually must be expertly placed in order to be effective.

SWITCH KICKS

A switch kick is a more advanced technique and requires a lot of bodily control and balance. The fundamental idea is to create a flurry of offense with your feet by issuing front or round kicks or knee strikes in rapid succession. This isn't one of the more practical Krav Maga techniques, but is a good exercise for students who have studied for a while and want to try something a bit more challenging. The switch kick is also a great way to keep up your conditioning. You'll get tired very quickly if you're not in peak shape.

Let's assume your switch kick consists of two round kicks, left foot first, then right. You'll need to jump in the air a little in order to execute the kicks in rapid succession. Don't try to kick too hard with the first kick; the first kick is more like your jab or set-up strike. Bring the first kick to the point of contact without swinging your hip, just use your leg. For the second kick, you're going to go full power with both the hip and the leg swing. Don't jump too high in the air or you'll make yourself too vulnerable to counter attack. Get just enough air to allow a seamless transition from one kick to the other. You're not going to be able to do this properly without hours upon hours of practice. To drill, forego the jump and just place your first foot on the target area (the lower portion of a heavy bag will work fine), bend your knees, and jump slightly while you swing your opposite hip *and* leg to connect with your second foot at maximum power. This exercise will prepare you to execute full aerial switch kicks in the future.

KNEE STRIKES

Colloquially known in fighting circles as "fight enders," knee strikes are close-range attacks that can deliver bone-crushing blows to an opponent. The knee is one of the body's hardest surfaces and can be a great weapon, especially in confined areas like hallways.

fig. 15 - Knee Strike

The best way to deliver a knee strike is to grab your opponent by the the tricep with one hand and the shoulder (same side) with the other hand, then bring the knee upwards while driving the opponent's torso towards your hip as shown in *figure 15*. This combination of force will create a massive impact. Before striking you should make sure the muscles in your striking leg are tight from your ankle to your glutes. Using this grip and strike method, you can alternate your target from the stomach to the solar plexus to the face. Alternating your knee strikes to target different areas of your opponent's body will prevent him from being able to block or counter you.

chapter five
PUNCH & STRIKE DEFENSE

As you will quickly learn while training in Krav Maga, there is constant emphasis on the simultaneous execution of offense and defense. The defensive maneuvers in Krav Maga are custom-tailored to expose immediate opportunities for powerful and devastating offense. In this chapter, we're going to review in detail Krav Maga tactics that can be applied when defending against common strikes and punches.

COUNTER ATTACKING GRABS & HOOK PUNCHES

One of the most common street-fighting scenarios you may encounter is someone trying to push you or grab you by the shirt. If he's feeling lucky, he may also try to sucker punch you with a hook punch. To quickly neutralize this type of attack, use your tricep to entangle your opponent's pushing arm. Do this by bringing your arm across and over your opponent's arm to trap the arm, then, with the arm still under your control, grab his shoulder. Meanwhile, bring your free arm into a half-guard to protect against a possible hook punch from your opponent's opposite hand. If you've successfully trapped the pushing arm, you will be able to force your opponent to the ground by controlling his shoulder joint. If need be—while controlling the shoulder joint and forcing your opponent to bend down—you can deliver a sequence of hard knees to your opponent before driving him all the way down to the ground.

Another way to generally protect against an unarmed hook punch is to use your forearm and bicep as a shield. Bend your arm all the way at the elbow and pull your arm up next to your head with your hand clenching the back of your neck. This is not the preferred method of defense, as it doesn't immediately lend itself to new offense, but can be useful if you are caught by surprise outside your fighting stance. If you use this defense, make sure you get your hand all the way behind your head. You don't want to get caught trying to protect the side of your face with just your hand. If your opponent makes impact with your hand not only will he still be directing a heavy impact into your face, but he may damage your hand as well. Your bicep area and forearms provide much better protection. This type of block is not mean to be overused, as it leaves your lower body and ribs exposed, a weakness that an attacker will quickly exploit.

Counter outside punches by using your other arm in a quick punch, like a hammer fist to the collarbone. True to the Krav Magra style, the first counter strike should land perfectly in synch with your blocking of the opponent's outside punch and should be followed by a tirade of follow-up offense. It's very important that your first counter hits lighting fast, because after you block the outside punch, you will be in range of your opponent's other hand and only in a half-guard.

When you drill, practice the blocking motion with the arm and the counterpunch at the same time, followed by a succession of knee strikes.

DEFENDING & COUNTERING STRAIGHT PUNCHES

The difference between defending a straight punch and defending an outside punch like a hook is that you really can't stop the punch from progressing, all you can do is redirect the punch so it doesn't reach its intended target.

To redirect a straight punch, think of your hand as ramp that you're going to use to skew the trajectory of the oncoming punch. Try to use as little movement as possible, simply positioning your hand in such a way that the assailant's punch is forced into a new angle. You can accompany the misdirection with a slight head dodge. For example, if you're misdirecting a left-handed cross inwardly, you can move your head outward just enough to avoid any chance of impact. You don't want to exert too much motion to counter a punch, and you certainly don't want to grab your opponent's arm. The point of Krav Maga is to be always on the cusp of a debilitating tirade of offense that will neutralize your foe unconditionally. Your blocks should be highly efficient and put you in a position to respond immediately with your own counter. Generally speaking, when blocking a straight punch, you're best off maneuvering the punch inward and away while you move slightly outward to commence your counter attack. This way, you won't have to worry about any offense coming from your opponent's other hand.

DEFENDING THE UPPERCUT

Uppercuts are usually attempted at close quarters, and the best shield you have against them is your forearm. It may be tempting to try and divert the uppercut the same way you divert straight punches, by reaching down with your palms and intercepting the punch or changing its trajectory. But this, unfortunately, will leave your face open to attack. Keep your hands in the same fighting-stance position that you'd use as your baseline positioning for other blocks and counters. Lower the elbow and use the forearm to defend against the incoming uppercut. As the punch comes in, lean with the elbow and direct the punch away from you. Your opponent's body is going to be turning while executing the uppercut, so be sure to use this movement against your opponent by redirecting his uppercut inside and away from you. Since his body is going to be turned after a successful block, you will have the opportunity to engage in all manners of close quarter counterattack including elbow strikes, crosses and straight punches.

DEFENSE WHEN MOUNTED BY AN OPPONENT

When your attacker is on top of you, straddling you and burdening you with all of his body weight (as shown in *figure 16* on the following page), it's important to know exactly how to defend yourself. From the **mount position** your attacker has free reign to strike your face, and you are not in a position to strike back with any force.

First, protect your face. Your best shot at blocking an incoming tirade of strikes while mounted is to place your hands on top of your head so your forearms form a cage around your face. This will allow you to block or compromise a couple of incoming strikes but is by no means a complete defense. You have to get out of this position and fast. In order to get out of this position, you have to use your hips. To start, bring your feet up as close to your butt as possible. You're going to thrust upwards with your hips with all your force to try and dislodge your attacker. It's important, however, that you also direct your attacker either left or right. If you just thrust up with your hips, you may dislodge your attacker, but you will only thrust him forward, and he will be able to quickly reassert his mount.

When you thrust out with your hips, you need to simultaneously roll one way or the other, finishing the movement on one of your hips. You can also grip either side of your attackers abdomen to throw your attacker one way or the other in conjunction with the hip thrust. You will send your attacker away from you and off to one side, giving yourself an opportunity to regain your footing.

Another way to escape the mount is to buck the opponent forward with your hips, not favoring any left or right direction as was essential to the previous method. Once the opponent is directed forward, he will catch and stabilize himself with his hands just beyond your head. In one smooth and continuous motion, use both of your hands to grab his left hand by the wrist and pull it down tight to your body. Trap his foot by placing your own right foot on the outside of the assailant's left foot. Buck your hips again and this time roll over on top of your opponent using the technical leverage you just created.

In Krav Maga, you are always aiming to unequivocally neutralize the opponent as quickly and as devastatingly as possible. To this end, once you have turned the tables on your opponent, immediately start in with a series of offensive strikes. Deliver a couple debilitating eye strikes. Grab your opponent's legs and spread them as you get back on your feet, and deliver a hard stomp to the groin.

Finally, as an alternative to grabbing your opponent's wrist after the forward buck, you can use your right elbow to collapse his left arm down and inward (or vice versa). Immediately grab your opponent with both hands around the upper back, trap the foot with your leg, buck your hips and turn him over.

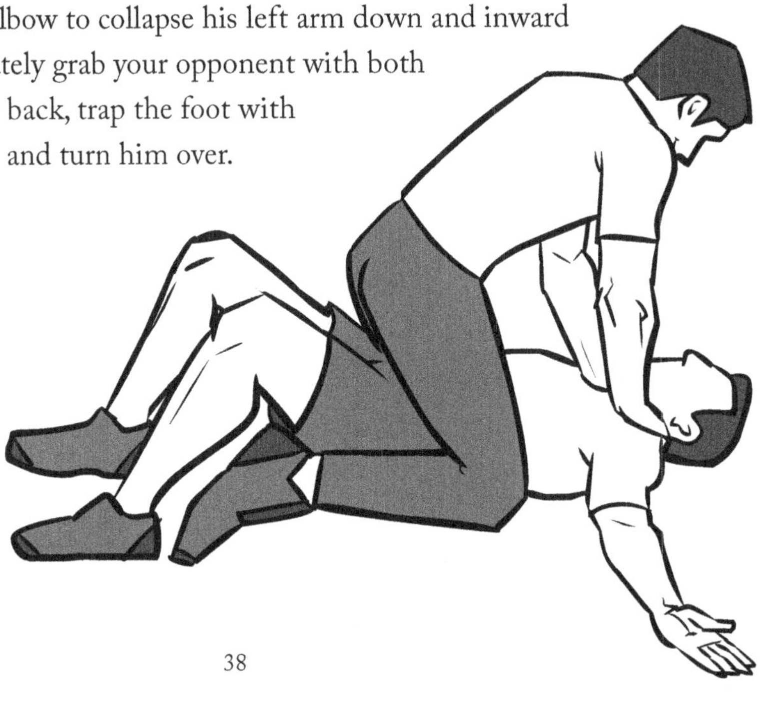

fig. 16 – Mount Position

DEFENDING ELBOW STRIKES

Defending elbow strikes is one of the easiest defenses to learn because the motion should be instinctual. Since effective elbow strikes are delivered at close quarters, the proper defense is to raise your arm and block vertically with your palm or forearm. True to Krav Maga principles you should immediately explode back with elbows and other offenses of your own. Choose your counter strike based on the position in which you're left after blocking your opponent's strike. If you need to use the same arm you used to block to deliver your counter, then consider using the eye strike or the hammer fist, as these attacks can be delivered quickly.

If possible, the best way to block the elbow is to avoid the elbow. Do this by sidestepping your opponent's attack and driving his elbow forward and past you. This should end up behind your opponent and in a position to get a good attack off on his neck, back, leg or another vulnerable area.

THE 360-DEGREE DEFENSE

In Krav Maga, there are **outside defensive** maneuvers and **inside defensive** maneuvers. A good way to learn the difference between the two is to envision a pole coming forward out of each of your shoulders, parallel to the ground. When you block an attack by moving your arms from the outside to the inside (between the two poles), you are forming an inside defense. When you block an attack by moving your arms from the inside to the outside (beyond one of the poles), you are forming an outside defense. The Krav Maga 360-degree offense focuses on outside defenses. It is designed to mitigate surprise attacks that come at you from unexpected outside angles, the type of attacks you'd likely encounter on the street. The 360-degree defense is based on instinctual reactions. Our basic reaction to a surprise attack is to raise our arms up to our face, palms outward to block the incoming blow. Krav Maga turns this instinctual defensive reaction into an offensive reaction that can immediately give you an advantage in a street fighting situation.

When you train on the Krav Maga 360-degree defense, you work on defending seven specific areas around the body. Imagine again the two poles proceeding from your shoulders, parallel to the ground. Now imagine an oval, roughly the size of your body, forming a tube through which the poles travel. This oval represents the areas—above you, to your side, and from below—from which a surprise *outside* attack may come. There are seven attack positions identified in Krav Maga training beginning with position 1— over head stab—and ending with position 7—underhand stab. Positions 2 through 6 denote the other positions on the longer, lateral curve of the oval, everywhere from your thigh to shoulder-length on either side of your body. When you train in Krav Maga, you learn to form effective blocks and counter attacks to aid you when attacked from any of these seven outside positions.

Blocking and countering effectively depends on your knowledge of and adherence to certain core Krav Maga principles. You should strive to make *wrist-to-wrist* contact with your opponent's incoming arm strike or stabbing motion. Make sure you have your elbow bent and that you're not hunching to make the block, extending yourself to a point at which you sacrifice balance. Use the blade of your forearm to exert strong pressure against the attack *(figure 17)*. It's important that you exert pressure when blocking and not just hold your arm out and hope for the best. Make the block before your assailant is able to generate a lot of power. It's easier to make the block at an earlier point of the opponent's striking or stabbing motion rather than at a later point. True to the principles of Krav Maga, a well-placed block must be accompanied by a counter-attack. You should burst forward into your block and counter-attack with an inside punch, elbow, kick or knee depending the threat.

fig. 17 - 360 Degree Defense

chapter six
DEFENDING ARMED ATTACKS

In Krav Maga, the name of the game is survival on the street. Much of your training will involve simulations of weapon-based attacks. To become even modestly proficient in these or any Krav Maga techniques, you must seek out a competent trainer.

Engaging an armed opponent is incredibly dangerous and should be attempted only as a last resort. Krav Maga teaches that avoidance is your first and best line of defense. RCAT is a useful acronym for the general principles of defending against armed attacks. R is for "redirect." In most any armed attack, you're going to redirect your assailant's weapon. C is for "control." After you redirect, you're going to take control of the weapon, usually by grabbing the assailant's wrist. A is for "attack." Per the overarching Krav Maga teachings, a good defense is a good offense. And T is for "take away." The final step to ending a weapon threat is to remove the weapon from the assailant's possession. Defending against weapons attacks is something you'll practice frequently during Krav Maga training. Usually, during training, plastic dummy weapons will be used to help you master these potentially life-saving techniques.

NOTE

It's important to remind the reader here that the techniques prescribed in this chapter must be drilled and practiced for months *or even years* before they are effective. Reading a book does not endow you with a skill, but only offers you a blue print and head start for your training.

DEFENSE AGAINST A DOWNWARD KNIFE STAB

Defending a downward stab begins with the fundamental three principles of the *360-degree defense* described in detail in Chapter 5: *wrist-to-wrist* contact, elbow bent, and drive through with pressure and a counterattack. For a counter attack, since you're defending from position 1 and presumably blocking with your left arm against a right-handed thrust, use your right arm for a quick, hard cross punch. Your offense will distract your opponent and allow you to use your wrist and the blade of your arm to drive your opponent's hand down and back. Keep the weapon-wielding arm behind the shoulder. If it's in front of the shoulder, then your opponent will have the power of his arm, shoulder, and body weight to use in a potentially devastating attack to your stomach. Keep the weapon beyond his shoulder and you minimize your chances of being stabbed in the stomach. Get a good grip on the wrist of the assailant's weapon-wielding hand, and use two quick knee strikes to the stomach to debilitate your opponent further.

Now you're ready to disarm the assailant. Begin by bringing your assailant's weapon-wielding arm towards you. Turn his wrist inward as you do so that the weapon is turned away from you. Hold tight to the wrist and push back on his hand to weaken his grip on the weapon. Quickly rake the weapon away with your right hand. From here a strong front kick can be used to put distance between you and the assailant.

DEFENSE AGAINST A STRAIGHT KNIFE STAB

A straight knife attack comes in a thrusting motion at your chest or midsection. In order to avoid this attack it's important to apply a combination of blocking, dodging and countering. One of the most dangerous aspects of the straight stab is that a poorly conceived diversion can easily open up an opportunity for your assailant to stab you in an alternate manner.

Redirect an incoming straight stab with your left arm. Use an outside-in motion while turning your body inwards towards your opponents arm. You must grab your assailant's wrist, preventing him from pulling back suddenly and cutting your arm and hand. When you grab his wrist, don't leave your elbow up or you will give your assailant direct access to your abdomen for a slice attack; instead, keep your elbow down, forming a wall with your arms to protect your body. All of this should be achieved in a quick, continuous motion and should be immediately followed by offense, a couple straight punches to distract your opponent. When he's distracted by your offense, compromise the wrist and rake the knife from his hands aggressively.

DEFENSE AGAINST AN UPWARD KNIFE STAB

An upward stab attack with a knife *(position 7)* means your opponent attacks with an upswing of the arm into your leg, groin or stomach. Again, you'll need to expertly combine, dodge, block, and counterattack defenses.

Start by sidestepping the upward knife stab while simultaneously grabbing your assailant's knife-wielding hand by the wrist. Make sure your hand is covering his thumb so he doesn't transfer possession of the knife to his other hand. Isolate the weapon-wielding hand by pinning down to his body as you attack him high with your punches. Pull the weapon hand out from the body and deliver a front kick to the groin. With your assailant stunned, use both hands to twist the wrist upwards with tremendous pressure, forcing your opponent to the ground. Deliver a hard stomp to the head, and you should have no trouble raking the weapon from your assailant's hand.

DEFENSE AGAINST A KNIFE ATTACK FROM BEHIND

Having a knife at your back is not a good position, and you should do everything in your power to get yourself to safety through some other means rather than by force. To defend against an attacker who is holding a knife at you from behind, you're going to roll around to your left while simultaneously entangling your assailant's arm. Do this by threading your left arm, opposite your assailant's knife hand, beneath and then above your assailant's knife-wielding arm. Immediately. With your assailant's weapon-arm under your control, bring your right arm up and across your opponent and grab him on the back over his right shoulder. Deliver a couple knee strikes to put your opponent on defense and give yourself a chance to gain full wrist control. Grab the wrist with your other hand so that you now have two hands on the wrist, and rotate your assailant's wrist, forcing him to bend forward at his waist. From here you should be able to rake out the knife and proceed with neutralizing your assailant.

KNIFE TO THE THROAT DEFENSE (FROM THE FRONT):

The following sequence can help you thwart a situation in which an assailant pushes a knife to your throat and threatens you. As always, if there is anything you can do to avert the conflict without engaging the opponent violently, please do so.

Move away from the knife—bend at the waist and knees while bringing a hand up to grab the assailant's weapon-hand wrist. Combine this movement with a simultaneous straight punch. Placement of the punch is not important here as long as you're forcing your assailant into a defensive disposition. After the punch, reach upwards and across your assailant with your free hand, grab him by the back of the shoulder and deliver a knee to the groin. Elevate the hand high and turn the arm, forcing your opponent to bend over while you deliver a solid straight kick to the face. Once your opponent is dazed you will be able push the wrist forward with your free hand, rake the weapon away and put some space between you and your assailant.

DEFENDING AGAINST A GUN THREAT FROM THE FRONT

The most common gun-defense situation is the robbery at gunpoint, when an assailant holds a gun up, aims at your face and demands something, usually money. As always, if you can defuse the situation by giving the assailant your money or your watch, then you will have successfully implemented Krav Maga techniques by simply staying alive. If you have given the assailant everything you have to give him and he is still pointing a gun at you, an attack may be imminent.

Like knife attacks, defending against gun attacks involves the *RCAT principle*. You're most vulnerable against a gun when you have your hands up. When you have your hands up at head level, your assailant will have an easier time catching and preempting any movement you attempt. All he has to do is pull a trigger. The best time to initiate your defense is when your hands are low. Movements from lowered hands are more stealthy and more apt to catch an assailant off guard.

To defend against a gun threat from the front, quickly grab your assailant's gun by the front barrel and redirect the aim of the weapon downward while you throw two or three hard punches with your opposite hand. With your assailant dazed, bring your punching hand to the top corner of the gun and grip it over the hammer. Twist the gun fast with both hands, rotating the barrel opening towards your assailant, who, if he still has his trigger finger in place, will likely have his finger broken by your hard twist. Rip the gun away and create distance between yourself and the assailant.

DEFENDING AGAINST A GUN FROM BEHIND

As with the knife at the back scenario, having a gun pointed at the back of your head is an incredibly compromising situation and not one that you want to try and physically resist if some other means of survival is available to you.

If you've exhausted all other options, then you first want to turn your head slightly, if possible, to get whatever visual you can on the exact position of the weapon. Move your body and reposition your feet to get out of the line of the gun barrel as quickly as possible. Rotate your body and trap the assailant's gun-wielding arm by lifting your left arm over and then under his gun-wielding arm. Turn your torso inward, bringing the assailant's arm close to your chest as you deliver a knee or two to the midsection, followed by an elbow across the face *(figure 18)*. With your assailant dazed and the gun arm still in your control, use your free hand to grab and rotate the weapon. Keep the gun pointed to the ground to avoid a misfiring that will endanger civilians. To disarm your assailant, grip the gun, bend it in a way that will allow it to slide off the assailants trigger finger.

fig. 18 - Gun Defense

45

STICK, CLUB, OR BAT DEFENSE

In order to defend against a stick attack you must quickly shoot in towards your assailant's shoulder as soon as he coils it back. Keeping your head down, lunge with your dominant foot and extend two arms *together* above the shoulder of the assailant's weapon-wielding arm. This will immediately limit the range of motion your assailant has available for his strike. Immediately wrap your arm around your opponent's weapon arm, trapping it.

Use your free arm to either strike your opponent with some quick punches, or grab him over the shoulder and deliver a couple knee strikes *(figure 19)*. Once he is stunned, bring your free hand back to the stick. Rotate your body towards the opponent's weapon-wielding arm, and use both hands to twist the weapon away using your hip and legs to power the rotation of your body. When the weapon is in your control, rotate back towards your opponent, striking him high with the butt of the weapon.

As with all defenses against armed opponents, they must be practiced until you can execute them in a quick and fluid motion.

NOTE

If your opponent is using his right arm to strike with the weapon, then you will use your left arm to trap, and vice versa

fig. 19 - Stick, Club, or Bat Defense

chapter seven
DEFENDING AGAINST KICKS & KNEE STRIKES

Avoiding and countering your opponent's kicks and knee strikes is a fundamental element of unarmed combat. Here are some Krav Maga techniques to apply when defending kicks.

DEFENDING AGAINST FRONT KICKS

Front kicks come hard and fast, so you need to be reflexive, quick, and accurate with your movements. To defend against an incoming front kick, sidestep the kick and move forward, using the blade of your forearm to parry the kick. Turn your body inward towards the opponent as you move. As you quickly sidestep and parry the kick, use your non-parrying hand to punch your opponent's face. Ideally you will strike him while he is standing on one foot, and then follow up with a punch from the opposite hand.

DEFENDING AGAINST ROUND KICKS

There are a few ways you can defend against round or "roundhouse" kicks. Unlike front kicks, round kicks require more movement and more time to execute, leaving the kicker with a wider window of vulnerability. The first technique to use when defending a round kick is fairly simple: dodge the kick by stepping backwards

NOTE

If you're facing your opponent squarely in fighting stance, and he is kicking with his right foot, sidestep to the left and parry with your right forearm. If he is kicking with his left foot, sidestep to the right and parry with your left forearm.

and then blitz forward to attack at the tail end of your opponent's kicking motion. If the round kick is coming in at a height below your waist, then you can lift your leg to block, using the tough musculature of your calf or thigh as a shield.

For higher round kicks, catch your opponent's leg in mid-motion. Be sure to use your whole arm; wrap it around the leg, holding it just below the knee. Use your other hand to immediately strike or grab your opponent's face. While still holding your opponent's leg and face, step forward and between your opponent's legs, threading your leg around his base. Still holding the leg, push forward hard on the opponent's face, taking out his base leg and forcing him to the floor. This will permit you time to create space between yourself and your opponent.

Finally, simply using your basic guard can be an effective way to mitigate roundhouse kicks while preparing your counter. Remember the principles of an effective guard: hands up, chin tucked, and elbows down. Per Krav Maga technique, you should always be on the offense. Stay aggressive by moving forward into the kicks. Block and immediately land punches before your opponent's kicking leg returns to the ground.

DEFENDING AGAINST SIDE KICKS & BACK KICKS

Similar to the front kick, the side kick comes in fast and straight and requires cat-like reflexes and agility to deflect and counter. Watch your opponent's fighting style for any signals that he may unknowingly be using to telegraph his kicks. To defend a side kick, side step the kicking foot, while using the blade of your forearm to parry if needed, and quickly reposition yourself to the side or rear of your opponent. Proceed with hard counters to the neck, groin, or the back of the head.

When defending against a back kick in which you are standing behind your opponent and he's thrusting his foot back towards you, step quickly to the side and catch the foot at ankle level. Extend the kick's movement, forcing your opponent to land with his feet spread far apart, leaving him extremely vulnerable to a front kick counter to the groin.

DEFENDING AGAINST KNEE ATTACKS

The biggest disadvantage of the knee attack is that the attacker will normally be using one or both of his hands to grip the opponent by the neck or back in order to best position his knee strikes. This leaves your hands free to intercept or check the incoming knee strikes. To do this, use open hands, specifically outward palms, to intercept your opponent's knee strikes. You may be naturally inclined to try and block the strike at the knee itself, but work on blocking the movement higher up the thigh. If you apply a bit of responsive pressure as the thigh is being driven upwards, you can easily disrupt or neutralize the strike. Furthermore, blocking the motion at the thighs rather than the knees provides a smooth transition into an uppercut counter. If you're looking for a quicker counter, then use one arm to block the incoming knee and use the other to deliver an immediate strike to the groin or stomach. You can also block and grab rather than block and strike. Do this by quickly wrapping your non-blocking hand around the leg your opponent is using to execute his knee strikes. Duck down and chop out the opponent's base leg to take him to the ground, where you can visit him with all manner of devastating offense.

chapter eight
HOW TO FALL & FIGHT ON THE GROUND

The reality of a lot of real-world and street fighting is that it happens on the ground. In this chapter we'll explore some Krav Maga techniques that will help you stay safe and in control when taking it to the floor.

HOW TO FALL

Depending on the direction you are following, different techniques can help you minimize the damage you will take.

When backwards falls, you want to spread the impact widely across your body to avoid letting any given area absorb too much shock, and you want to avoid the back of your head hitting the ground, as this is the most dangerous aspect of the backwards fall. To prepare yourself for the backwards fall, start by falling from a squatting position. Spread your arms out and down at 45-degree angles as you fall. Keep your chin tucked. This will move your head forward and prevent it from striking the ground during or after the fall. After you've practiced several falls from a squatting position, practice falling from a standing position.

Like the backwards fall, the side fall should be practiced first from a sitting position. Aim to distribute the weight of your fall across the largest possible area. Stick out your arm on the side to which you're falling and try to land with your arm extended to a 45-degree angle. Hit the floor with the entire line of your arm. Avoid making pointed ground contact with the elbow or shoulder. After you are comfortable with the side fall from a sitting position, try doing it from a squatting position. From the squatting position, you'll want to work in your leg, trying to force it to land as evenly as possible on the surface. After you're comfortable practicing the fall in a squatting position, start practicing from a standing position using the same techniques. To simulate the fall from a standing position, sweep your right leg in front of your left leg and fall to the right. Don't be afraid to attack the ground as you fall to ensure an even impact, and remember to always keep your chin tucked when you fall.

GROUND DEFENSIVE POSITIONS

Given that Krav Maga is so offense-centric, finding yourself on the ground is not usually considered to be a good position. Nonetheless, it's an inevitable and common situation in a real fight; therefore Krav Maga has some techniques to help you stay safe on the floor.

Start by lifting your head up so that there are several inches of distance between the back of your head and the floor. Having your head up also allows you to keep your vision locked onto your opponent. Keep your guard up to protect your face and upper body. Have one foot in the air and the other on the floor. Use the foot on the floor to position your body. Your other foot can be used to strike. Use your striking foot to deliver a straight foot from the ground and to create distance between you and your opponent and give yourself a chance to return to your feet as quickly as possible. If, while in your ground defensive position, you find your opponent at your side, then you can deliver a round kick by rolling your hips towards your opponent and kicking with your top leg. Remember the whole point of ground offense is to give yourself a chance to get back up so you can neutralize your opponent. When getting up, keep one arm in the *half guard* and use the other to help you regain your feet. If your opponent closes back in on you before you have a chance to get all the way up, then fall back quickly to the ground defensive position and strike again until you create another opportunity to ascend.

ESCAPING MOUNTED GROUND CHOKE HOLDS

If your opponent has you mounted and is gripping your neck in a one-handed choke with his other fist back and ready to strike, your first priority is to procure the safe passage of air back into your lungs. You must break the chokehold. You may be tempted in this situation to try and grab your assailant by the wrist to dislodge his hand, but you'll fare better if you use a little more technique. Take a free hand, tuck in your thumb and make a hook with your hand, then scoop under your assailant's hand from the inside of his grip between his forefinger and the thumb. At the same time, bring one of your feet up as close to your backside as possible and tighten it up against your assailant's leg. Deliver a strike with your free, non-hooked hand. You're not going to be able to strike with a lot of force since you will have none of your weight at your disposal. The purpose of the strike is mainly to distract your assailant as you prepare the next phase of your escape and counter. You're going to buck upwards and roll your opponent slightly to the side with your hips, and follow him through the roll until *you* are *over him* in a mount. Assuming he wraps you up tight in a scissor hold, you're going to escape by keeping your head low and pushing up with your palms under his chin. From here you'll drive back with your elbow and connect with the center of his thigh, breaking the scissor hold. Slide further down and spring backwards onto your feet, gripping each of your opponent's legs as you do so and pushing them laterally away from you so he doesn't have any chance for a good kick.

If your opponent has you in a mount position and is using both of his hands in a two-handed choke, your first step is to break the pressure by popping his elbows. You'll have both hands free. Bring both of your hands above your opponent's arms and strike at the inside of his elbows to loosen the hold while simultaneously using your hips to buck his body forward. From here you can execute the trap and roll technique that was discussed in detail in Chapter 5, in which you move your legs up close to your butt, use both hands to trap the opponents arm at the wrist, then roll him over.

ESCAPING THE GUARD POSITION

In the guard position, your opponent has you on the ground, has your body secured between his legs in a scissor lock, and has your head and upper body secured with his arms. To escape from this position, use both hands to push up towards your opponent's face and under his chin. This will force his arms to loosen or break their grip. Once the grip is compromised, strike at the groin and midsection, and then deliver a hard elbow to the thigh to compromise the scissor hold. Control the legs with your hands as you escape to your feet to avoid any retaliatory kicks.

conclusion

The execution of Krav Maga assumes a universe of high stakes. Imi Lichtenfeld created the system at a time when his life and the lives of the people in his community were constantly threatened and in a country that was on the verge of occupation and war. The techniques were refined in Palestine, an actual living, breathing warzone. Today, Krav Maga is extremely popular all over the world, and most of the civilian population that seeks out Krav Maga training is not braving anything close to the same environment in which it originated. Krav Maga is a practical and lethal fighting skill set, but hopefully not one that you will regularly have to employ.

As with other martial arts, fitness is a fantastic secondary goal for your training, *though your primary goal, of course, is self-defense.* Joining a Krav Maga training center can improve your physical fitness as well as boost your self-confidence, in addition to giving you the tools you need to stay safe in the most dangerous of situations.

glossary

Base Foot -
The foot that stays planted during a kick.

Fighting Stance -
A standing position that allows you to strike your attacker quickly and powerfully.

Full Guard -
Using both hands, forearms and arms to protect the face and upper body.

Half Guard -
Using only one hand, forearm, and arm to protect the face and upper body.

Guard (Grappling Position) -
A ground grappling position in which one fighter has his/her back to the ground and is attempting to control the other by using her legs to constrict him around the waist.

Neutral Stance -
Refers to normal standing position, not anticipating attack. This stance is used to practice being attacked by surprise.

Inside -
Refers to a motion of the arm, leg or weapon moving from outside the body center towards the body center.

Outside -
Refers to a motion of the arm, leg or weapon moving from the body center towards the outside of the body center.

Inside Defense -
Defending straight attacks aimed at the longitudinal center of the body, usually coming from the front.

Outside Defense -
Defending oblique attacks aimed at the body from an outside angle, which can come from the side, back, or front.

Kata -
An official non-combative system of exercises used in Karate or other martial arts consisting of poses, movements, and breathing patterns.

Mount Position -
A position in which an opponent/attacker is attempting to pin you to the ground by straddling your midsection (sitting on top of you).

Opponent/Attacker/Assailant -
Used interchangeably to describe the person you are engaging combat against.

RCAT Principle -
Used to summarize Krav Maga defense against armed attacks: Redirect, Control, Attack, Take Away.

Weapon -
Anything that can be used to do physical damage to an opponent, including body parts such as fist, leg, elbow, and knee.

about clydebank

We are a multi-media publishing company that provides reliable, high-quality and easily accessible information to a global customer base. Developed out of the need for beginner-friendly content that is accessible across multiple formats, we deliver reliable, up-to-date, high-quality information through our multiple product offerings.

Through our strategic partnerships with some of the world's largest retailers, we are able to simplify the learning process for customers around the world, providing them with an authoritative source of information for the subjects that matter to them. Our end-user focused philosophy puts the satisfaction of our customers at the forefront of our mission. We are committed to creating multi-media products that allow our customers to learn what they want, when they want and how they want.

ClydeBank Recreation is a division of the multimedia-publishing firm ClydeBank Media LLC. ClydeBank Media's goal is to provide affordable, accessible information to a global market through different forms of media such as eBooks, paperback books and audio books. Company divisions are based on subject matter, each consisting of a dedicated team of researchers, writers, editors and designers.

For more information, please visit us at :
www.clydebankmedia.com
or contact *info@clydebankmedia.com*

notes

STAY INFORMED

ClydeBank TECHNOLOGY | BLOG

Your Source for All Things Technology

Why Should I Sign Up for the Mailing List?

- Get a $10 ClydeBank Media gift card!
- Be the first to know about new products
- Receive exclusive promotions & discounts

Stay on top of the latest technology trends by joining our free mailing list today at:

www.clydebankmedia.com/technology-blog

Made in the USA
Middletown, DE
13 April 2019